For Mum, thank you for your support, advice, and library!
— S.F

To my parents, whose love and support help me grow.
— B.A

First edition published in 2025 by Flying Eye Books Ltd.
27 Westgate Street, London, E8 3RL.

Text © Sara Forster 2025
Illustrations © Bianca Austria 2025

Sara Forster has asserted her right under the Copyright, Designs and Patents Act, 1988, to be identified as the Author of this Work. Bianca Austria has asserted her right under the Copyright, Designs and Patents Act, 1988, to be identified as the Illustrator of this Work.

All rights reserved. No part of this publication may be reproduced or transmitted in any form or by any means, electronic or mechanical, including photocopying, recording or by any information and storage retrieval system, without prior written consent from the publisher.

Designed by Sarah Crookes

1 3 5 7 9 10 8 6 4 2

Published in the US by Flying Eye Books Ltd.
Printed in China on FSC® certified paper.

ISBN: 978-1-83874-891-3
Library ISBN: 978-1-83874-929-3
www.flyingeyebooks.com

Sara Forster   Bianca Austria

Watch Me Grow

Butterflies

Flying Eye Books

a butterfly flutter by...

but what is a butterfly?

A butterfly is a type of animal called an insect. Insects are small animals with a hard shell called an **exoskeleton**. You can find insects almost anywhere on Earth.

Butterflies, moths, bees, and ants are all types of insect.

Butterflies can look different from each other. They come in many shapes, colors, and sizes.

Some are big like the **Queen Alexandra's birdwing**. Its wings can reach as wide as 12 inches.

Others are very tiny, like the **western pygmy blue**, with wings less than 0.8 inches wide.

But no matter their size, they all have the same ...

Two feelers on its head.
These are called antennae and will help the butterfly find food.

A long, curly **tongue**.
It uses its tongue like a straw to sip its food.

An **abdomen**.

But how does a butterfly grow?

Butterflies start as tiny eggs.

A female butterfly carefully lays tiny, sticky eggs on the underside of leaves.

Butterfly eggs can be as small as the period at the end of this sentence. Most eggs are pale green or yellow.

Some eggs are small and round . . .

other eggs are smooth and thin . . .

and some eggs are laid in long chains.

Inside the egg, a caterpillar starts to grow. If you look really closely you can see a tiny caterpillar inside.

When it is ready to hatch, it starts to munch its way out of the egg.

First the little caterpillar eats the egg case …

Then it is ready to go through an even bigger change.

First the caterpillar finds a safe, shady place under a leaf or a branch.

It grips the branch with its back legs and then it attaches itself using a strand of silk.

Did you know *that caterpillars have special sticky feet that help them grip and move their long bodies.*

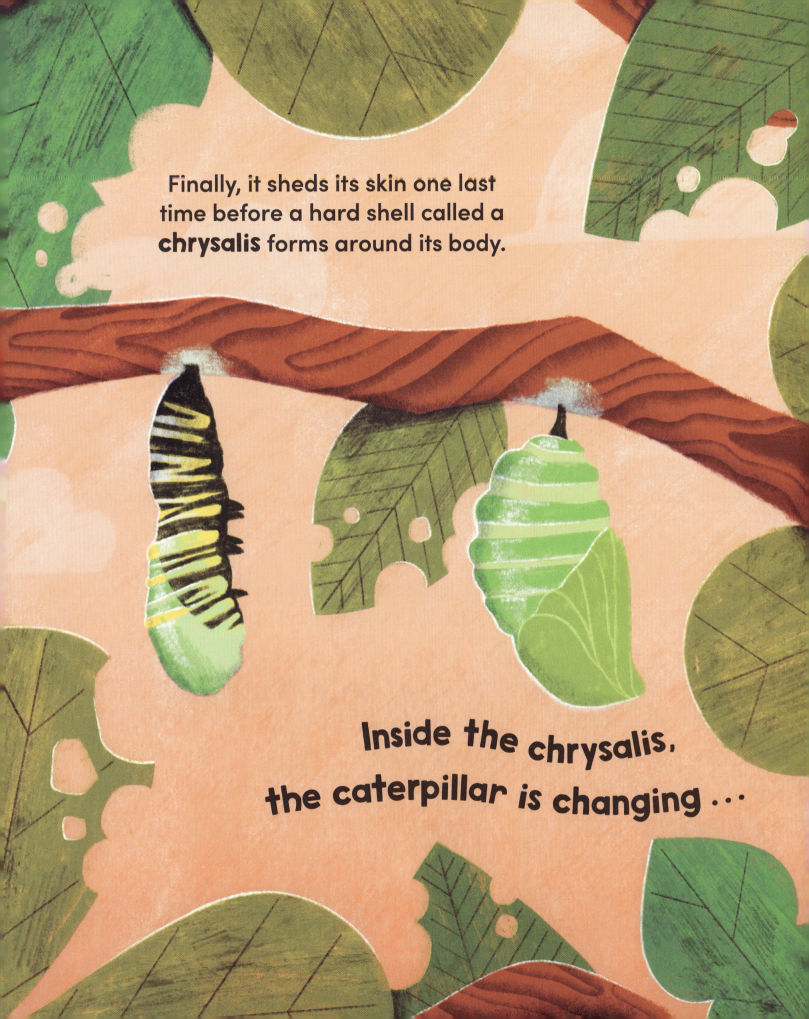

Finally, it sheds its skin one last time before a hard shell called a **chrysalis** forms around its body.

Inside the chrysalis, the caterpillar is changing...

it is time for the caterpillar to turn into a butterfly.

It transforms its whole body in a special way called **metamorphosis**.

After about 10 days the chrysalis begins to change color. The butterfly inside is getting ready to emerge.

to find food.

Most butterflies feed on **nectar**, a sweet, sugary liquid that flowers make. As the little butterfly flits from flower to flower, something special happens!

When a butterfly lands on a flower, **pollen** sticks to it. Pollen is a fine powder that helps a plant make seeds.

When the butterfly travels to the next flower, it spreads the pollen. This helps the flower make seeds.

One day these seeds will grow into new plants that will be home to the next generation of butterflies.

Did you know that other types drink the sugary juice inside fruit. But some butterflies have very strange taste . . . they like to eat animal poop!

Our butterfly must be careful though . . .

sometimes it needs to stay safe.

Butterflies have clever ways to hide and keep themselves safe from creatures that might want to eat them.

This monarch butterfly is **poisonous**. The bright colors and dots on their wings tell other animals: **"Don't eat me! I taste bad"**.

Other butterflies are good at hiding.

When a **peacock butterfly** rests with its wings closed, it looks just like a leaf that has turned brown and dry. This clever disguise helps them stay hidden and protected.

Can you spot the hidden peacock butterfly?

And some butterflies can be scary…

This **owl butterfly** has a pattern on its wings that looks just like an eye. These spots look like the eyes of a much larger and more dangerous animal.

Safe from danger…

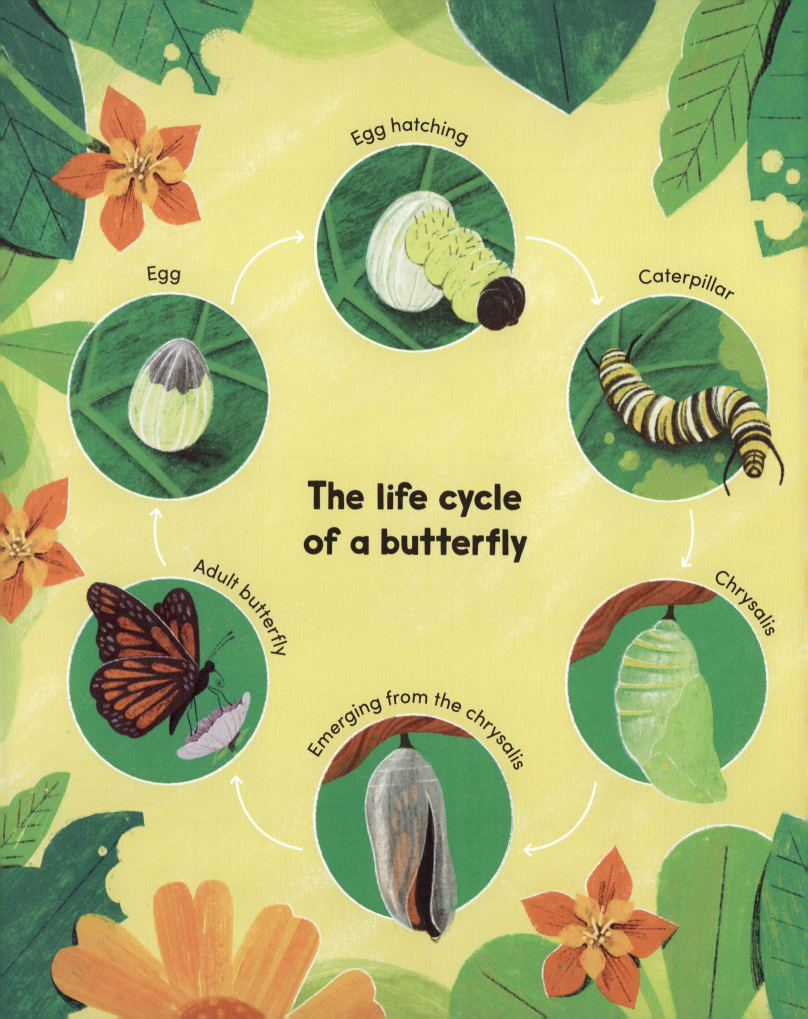

Glossary

Abdomen
The back part of the body of an insect.

Chrysalis
The hard cover a caterpillar makes around itself before it turns into a butterfly.

Exoskeleton
An exoskeleton is a hard covering that supports and protects the bodies of some types of animals.

Life cycle
The series of changes in the life of a living thing.

Metamorphosis
A complete change made by some living things, such as a caterpillar changing into a butterfly.

Nectar
A sweet liquid produced by plants, found in flowers.

Pollen
A fine, yellow powder found inside flowers.

Poisonous
A poisonous animal or insect can harm or kill another animal if eaten.

Thorax
The part of an insect's body between the head and the abdomen, to which the wings and legs are joined.